Drawing Is Fun!

DRAWING
DINOSAURS

Gareth Stevens
Publishing

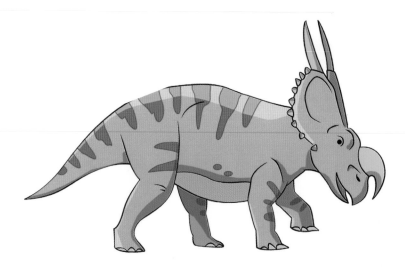

Please visit our website, www.garethstevens.com. For a free color catalog of all our high-quality books, call toll free 1-800-542-2595 or fax 1-877-542-2596.

Library of Congress Cataloging-in-Publication Data

Clunes, Rebecca.
Drawing dinosaurs / Rebecca Clunes.
    p. cm. — (Drawing is fun)
Includes index.
ISBN 978-1-4339-5944-8 (pbk.)
ISBN 978-1-4339-5945-5 (6-pack)
ISBN 978-1-4339-5942-4 (library binding)
1. Dinosaurs in art—Juvenile literature. 2. Drawing—Technique—Juvenile literature. I. Title.
NC780.5.C58 2011
743.6—dc22

2010052652

First Edition

Published in 2012 by
Gareth Stevens Publishing
111 East 14th Street, Suite 349
New York, NY 10003

Cartoon illustrations: Dynamo Limited
Text: Rebecca Clunes and Dynamo Limited
Editors: Anna Brett, Kate Overy, and Joe Harris
Design: Tokiko Morishima
Cover design: Tokiko Morishima

Picture credits: All 3D graphics supplied by Shutterstock, except for images on pages 6 and 8, supplied by iStockphoto.

Printed in China

CPSIA compliance information: Batch # AS11GS: For further information contact Gareth Stevens, New York, New York at 1-800-542-2595.

SL001841US

Contents

Apatosaurus

uh-pah-tuh-SOHR-uhs

This huge dinosaur was about 70 feet (21 meters) long.

Its neck was very long to reach its food.

It ate leaves and bushes growing near the ground.

It used its tail like a whip if a meat-eating dinosaur attacked it.

FUN FACTS ● FUN FACTS ● FUN FACTS ● FUN FACTS ● FUN FACTS

Apatosaurus lived in groups so the adults could keep the babies safe.

1. This shape is the body.

2. Make the neck long and smooth.

3. Put on the head and a long, strong tail.

4. It walks on four strong legs.

Tyrannosaurus rex

tuh-RA-nuh-SOHR-uhs REHKS

This dinosaur was about 20 feet (6 meters) tall.

Tyrannosaurus rex was one of the biggest meat eaters there has ever been.

It had very sharp teeth.

Its powerful legs helped it to run very fast.

FUN FACTS ● FUN FACTS ● FUN FACTS ● FUN FACTS ● FUN FACTS

Tyrannosaurus rex was so powerful it could crush bones with its teeth.

1. Draw this blobby shape.

2. Put a head at one end and a tail at the other.

3. Draw its eyes and mouth like this to make it look very fierce.

4. Give it sharp teeth and claws and a pair of strong legs.

Pteranodon

tuh-RA-nuh-dahn

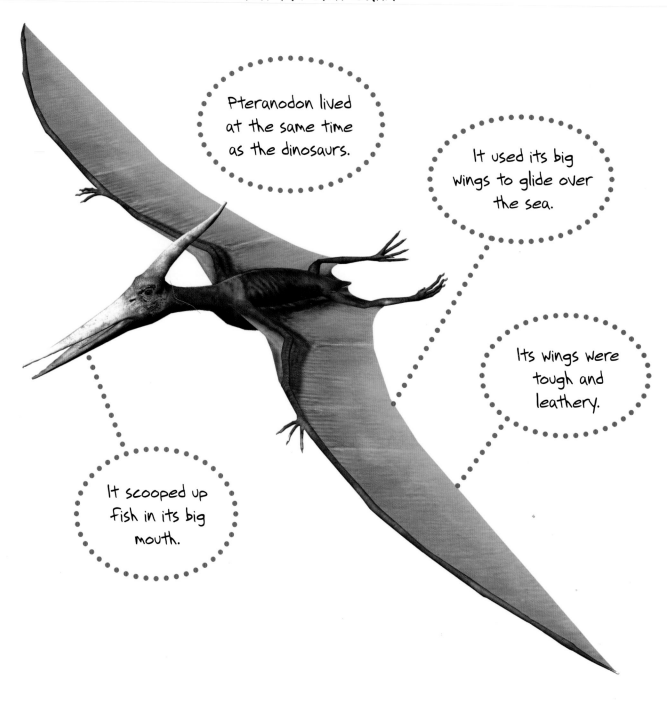

Pteranodon lived at the same time as the dinosaurs.

It used its big wings to glide over the sea.

Its wings were tough and leathery.

It scooped up fish in its big mouth.

FUN FACTS ● FUN FACTS ● FUN FACTS ● FUN FACTS ● FUN FACTS

From wing to wing, Pteranodon was 25 feet (nearly 8 meters) wide.

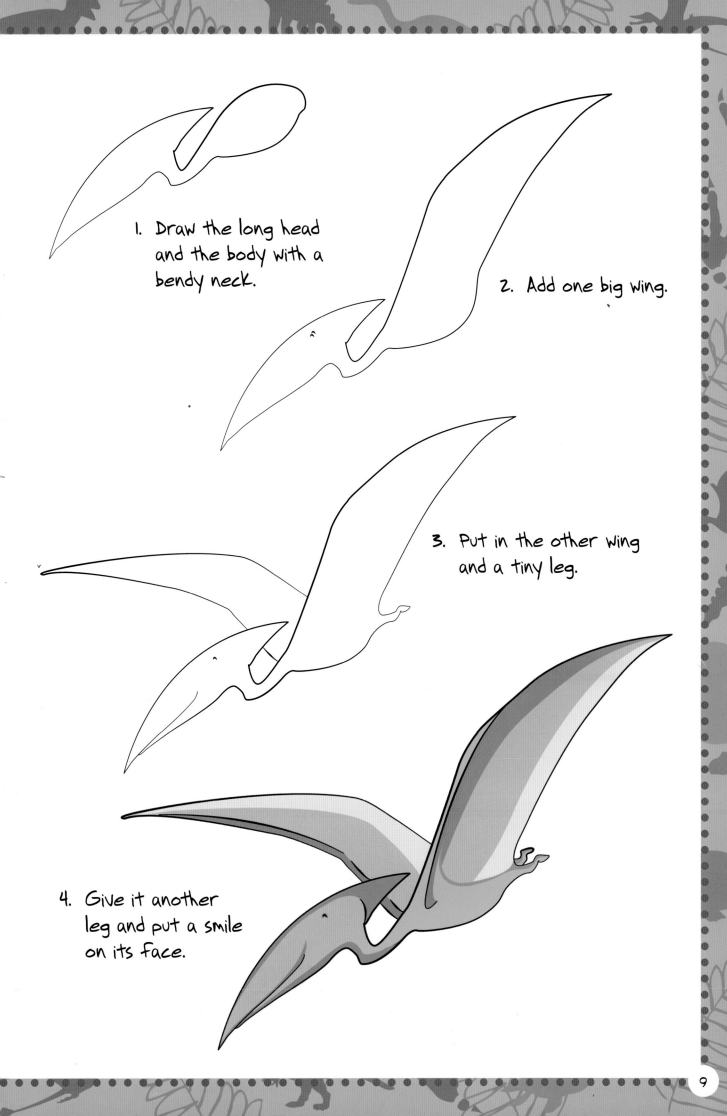

1. Draw the long head and the body with a bendy neck.

2. Add one big wing.

3. Put in the other wing and a tiny leg.

4. Give it another leg and put a smile on its face.

Triceratops

try-SEHR-uh-tahps

This dinosaur had two large horns and one smaller horn.

Triceratops was about 30 feet (9 meters) long.

It ate leaves and twigs.

It had strong legs to support its heavy body.

FUN FACTS ● FUN FACTS ● FUN FACTS ● FUN FACTS ● FUN FACTS

Triceratops had a bony plate around its neck to protect it from big meat eaters.

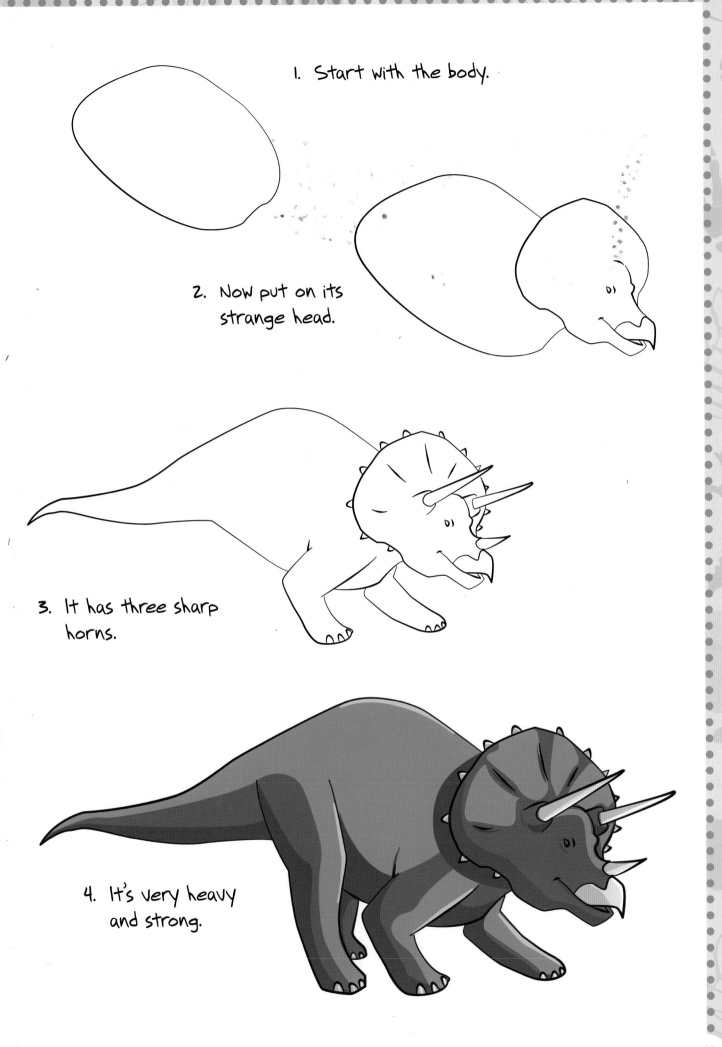

1. Start with the body.

2. Now put on its strange head.

3. It has three sharp horns.

4. It's very heavy and strong.

Archaeopteryx

ahr-kee-AHP-tuh-rihks

This was one of the first birds. It lived at the time of the dinosaurs.

It had feathers like a modern bird.

These claws helped it climb around in trees.

It could not fly well, but used its wings to glide.

FUN FACTS ● FUN FACTS ● FUN FACTS ● FUN FACTS ● FUN FACTS

Archaeopteryx was about the size of a pigeon.

1. Draw the body with a feathery tail.

2. Add the head and one large wing.

3. Now add the other wing.

4. Finish it off with legs and clawed feet.

Stegosaurus

steh-guh-SOHR-uhs

This dinosaur ate plants that grew near the ground.

Stegosaurus was about 30 feet (9 meters) long.

It had sharp spikes on its tail to protect itself.

Its front legs were much shorter than its back legs.

FUN FACTS ● FUN FACTS ● FUN FACTS ● FUN FACTS ● FUN FACTS

Stegosaurus had a very small brain. It was only about the size of a walnut.

1. Draw the body shape.

2. Add the thick neck and tiny head.

3. Now add the four legs.

4. It has big, flat pointed plates on its back.

Deinonychus

dy-NAH-nih-kuhs

This dinosaur had sharp eyes for spotting prey.

Its tail was used for balance as it ran.

It had large claws on its back feet.

Deinonychus was about 10 feet (3 meters) long.

FUN FACTS ● FUN FACTS ● FUN FACTS ● FUN FACTS ● FUN FACTS

Deinonychus hunted in groups. Together they could kill animals much bigger than themselves.

1. Draw a long body to start.

2. Add in the head.

3. Give it two small front legs.

4. Add the back legs, then draw its teeth and claws.

Parasaurolophus

pa-ruh-sohr-uh-LOH-fus

Parasaurolophus probably lived in groups.

This dinosaur had a huge crest on its head.

It ate pine needles and other tough leaves.

It could walk on two legs or four legs.

FUN FACTS ● FUN FACTS ● FUN FACTS ● FUN FACTS ● FUN FACTS

Parasaurolophus could blow through its crest. This made a loud, low noise.

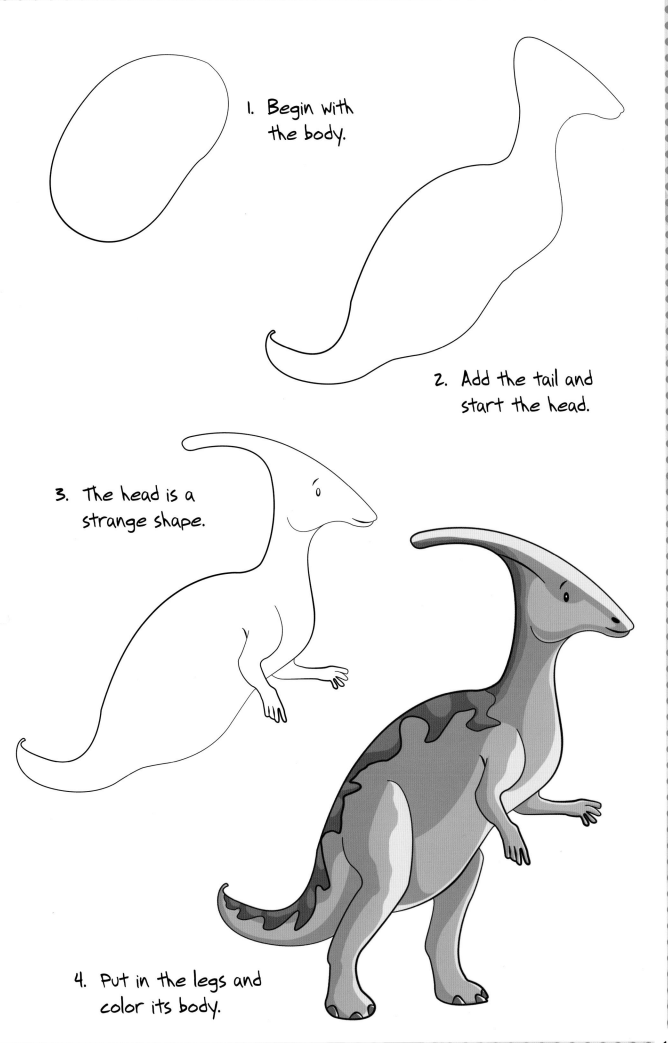

1. Begin with the body.

2. Add the tail and start the head.

3. The head is a strange shape.

4. Put in the legs and color its body.

Allosaurus

aa-luh-SOHR-uhs

Allosaurus was a meat-eating dinosaur.

Allosaurus was a big dinosaur, about 38 feet (almost 12 meters) long.

It had about 60 very sharp teeth.

It used its front claws to hold onto prey.

FUN FACTS ● FUN FACTS ● FUN FACTS ● FUN FACTS ● FUN FACTS

Allosaurus ate other dinosaurs. It tried to creep close to them. Then it suddenly attacked.

1. This shape makes the body and the tail.

2. Add the neck and head.

3. Short front arms and eyebrows are next.

4. Powerful back legs finish off this frightening animal.

Brachiosaurus

brah-kee-uh-SOHR-uhs

It used its long neck to reach the leaves at the top of trees.

This huge dinosaur was about 75 feet (23 meters) long.

It swallowed food without chewing it.

Its front legs were longer than its back legs.

FUN FACTS ● FUN FACTS ● FUN FACTS ● FUN FACTS ● FUN FACTS

A meat-eating dinosaur would not attack an adult Brachiosaurus. It was just too big!

1. A bumpy egg is the starting place for this dinosaur.

2. Give it a long neck and tail.

3. It has thick and powerful front legs.

4. Short back legs help keep this dinosaur on its feet.

Spinosaurus

spy-nuh-SOHR-uhs

Spinosaurus was a meat-eating dinosaur.

The "sail" on its back was taller than a person.

It snapped up fish with its sharp teeth.

It was more than 35 feet (11 meters) long.

FUN FACTS ● FUN FACTS ● FUN FACTS ● FUN FACTS ● FUN FACTS

Spinosaurus used its sail to keep warm. It stood so the sun shone on its sail. This warmed it up very quickly.

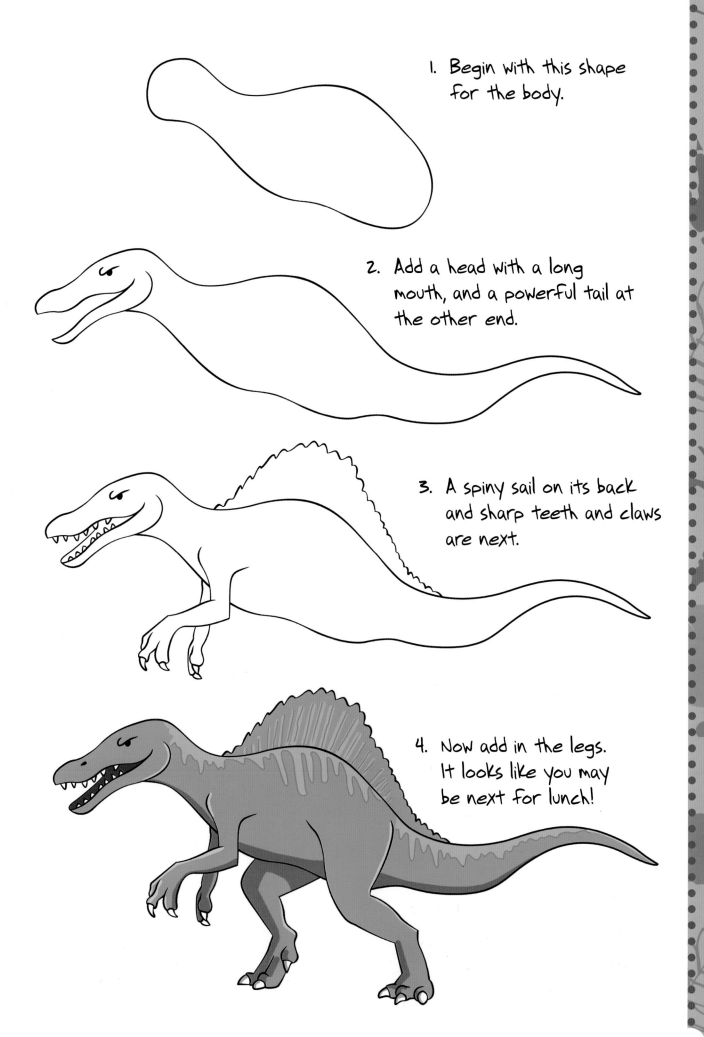

1. Begin with this shape for the body.

2. Add a head with a long mouth, and a powerful tail at the other end.

3. A spiny sail on its back and sharp teeth and claws are next.

4. Now add in the legs. It looks like you may be next for lunch!

Elasmosaurus

ih-laz-muh-SOHR-uhs

Elasmosaurus lived in the seas at the time of the dinosaurs.

Its long neck was used to reach down and snap up fish.

It used its big flippers to swim near the top of the water.

Its neck was as long as its body.

FUN FACTS ● FUN FACTS ● FUN FACTS ● FUN FACTS ● FUN FACTS

Although it spent most of its time in the water, Elasmosaurus breathed air and laid its eggs on land.

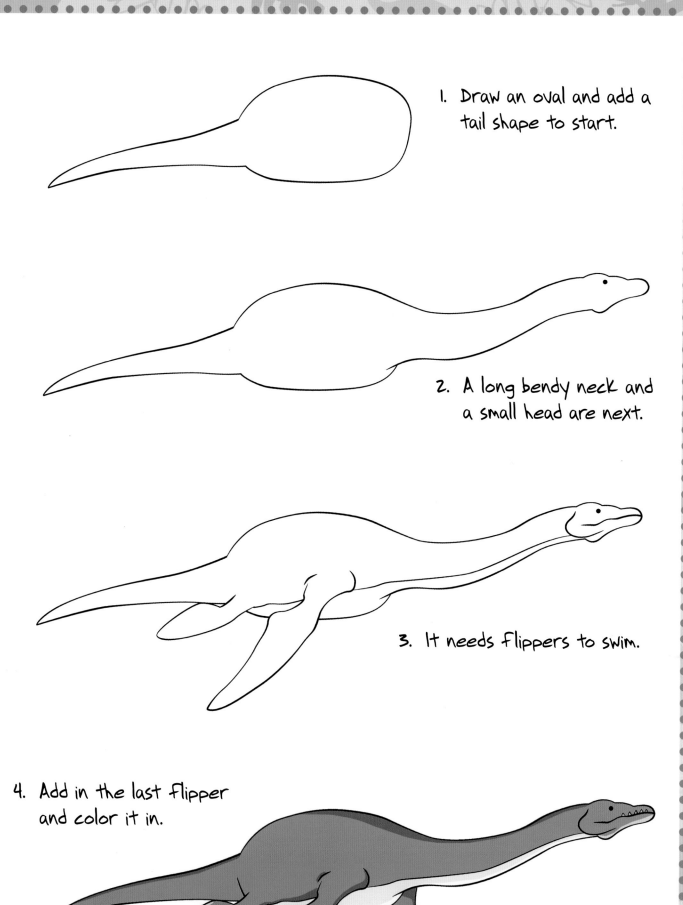

1. Draw an oval and add a tail shape to start.

2. A long bendy neck and a small head are next.

3. It needs flippers to swim.

4. Add in the last flipper and color it in.

Einiosaurus

eye-nee-uh-SOHR-uhs

This dinosaur ate plants.

It had a huge horn on its nose.

Einiosaurus had two horns to protect its neck.

Einiosaurus fossils have been found in North America.

FUN FACTS ● FUN FACTS ● FUN FACTS ● FUN FACTS ● FUN FACTS

Einiosaurus was about 20 feet (6 meters) long and it probably lived in groups.

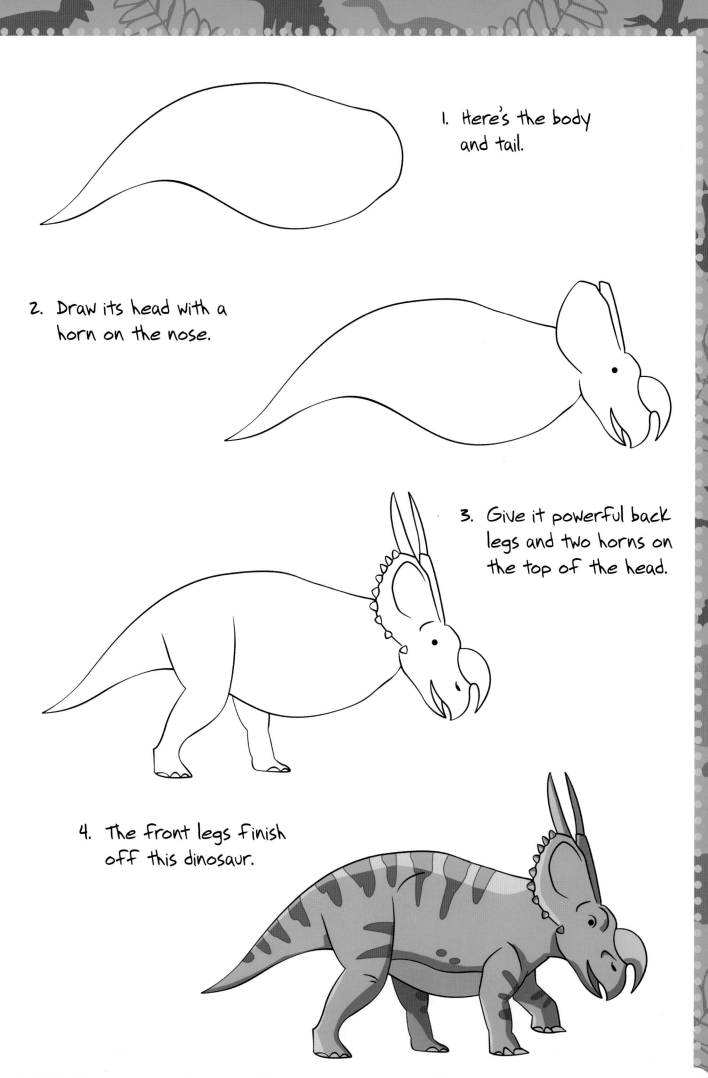

1. Here's the body and tail.

2. Draw its head with a horn on the nose.

3. Give it powerful back legs and two horns on the top of the head.

4. The front legs finish off this dinosaur.

Velociraptor

vuh-LAH-suh-rap-tuhr

This dinosaur was a fierce meat eater.

Its long legs made it a fast runner.

Its front claws were very sharp to grab prey.

It had long claws on its back feet.

FUN FACTS ● FUN FACTS ● FUN FACTS ● FUN FACTS ● FUN FACTS

A fossil has been found of a Velociraptor as it attacked a plant-eating dinosaur called Protoceratops.

1. Here's the body.

2. Draw the neck and a long pointy tail.

3. The head and the back legs are next.

4. Put in its front legs and its sharp teeth.

31

Glossary

balance to stand or move without falling over

bony with skin very near the bone

crest something standing out on top of an animal's head

flipper an animal's leg that is wide and flat, and made for swimming

fossil a rock that shows the shape of an animal or plant from millions of years ago

glide to float through the air for a long time without flapping wings

leathery like tough, thick animal skin

meat eater an animal that eats other animals

plate a hard, wide, flat part of the body

prey the animals that a meat eater kills

scoop to gather up a lot of food at once

spikes sharp points

whip to hit something as if with a long thin rope

Further Reading

Harpster, Steve. *Pencil, Paper, Draw! Dinosaurs.* Sterling, 2006.

Nishida, Masaki. *Drawing Manga Dinosaurs.* PowerKids Press, 2007.

Reisenauer, Cindy M. *Line By Line Everyone Can Draw Dinosaurs.* Puddle Jump Press, 2010.

Winterberg, Jenna and Fisher, Diana. *Watch Me Draw: Dinosaurs.* Walter Foster, 2006.

Index